NED CARTLEDGE

Ned Cartledge
11/17/88

NEXUS PRESS
ATLANTA, GEORGIA
1 9 8 6

Produced at Nexus Press
Printed in U.S.A.

Preface

My interest in Ned's wood relief carvings postdates knowing him personally. I suspect this is also the case for many people who have collected Ned's art. Even if one disagrees with his political and/or religious views (and in the South many do), it is hard not to be amused and convinced by the refreshingly direct observations in Ned's carvings and next to impossible to resist his views after talking with him.

But this is not reason enough to exhibit Ned's work at the Georgia Museum of Art and to support the publication of this book. Ned's work is good art. His ability to handle his medium—the drawing, carving, and coloring—is remarkable, all the more so because he has not attended art school or taken art courses. His use of shallow space, simple forms, and symmetrical compositions represents an unconscious affiliation with the broad trends of American folk art, with none of the pejorative connotations the term might imply.

Not only is Ned's ability to execute his craft excellent but the content of many of the pieces reflects a mind and spirit traveling a currently unpopular path. Ned's political pieces reflect his deeply-felt humanism in which he expresses century-old ideals through modern-day events taken from American mass culture. This is no senior citizen filling his twilight years whittling cutesy country scenes.

Ned's wood reliefs embrace the highest tenets of American folk art by expressing the American spirit of independence through humorous images beautifully crafted. His humility and gentleness make the most caustic satire seem obviously sensible. These have found favor with many people from all sections of the United States, which is all the more remarkable because Ned is a Southerner whose persona reflects southern traditions so often ridiculed by Americans from other regions.

I am very excited about having an exhibition of Ned's work at the Georgia Museum of Art and the concurrent publication of this book. Both are a well-deserved tribute to Ned as a person and fine artist.

Donald D. Keyes
Curator of American Painting
Georgia Museum of Art

Photograph: Elizabeth Turk

Ned Cartledge— Atlanta Folk Artist

Southern folk art is about as diverse an *oeuvre* as one could amass under a single rubric and still retain a germ of intellectual precision. When one speaks of Ned Cartledge as a quintessential southern folk artist, it probably calls for some explanation.

The southern states have traditionally fused a unique alchemy of religious fervor and social consciousness, which is notable among regionalisms of the U.S. Typically, that religious fervor is fundamentalist in flavor, and the social consciousness is conservative, but the generative power of this combination has been well understood since the Confederacy. The power of that prophetic tradition remains alive and well in today's South, but folk artist Ned Cartledge probably represents one of its most liberal and entertaining voices.

In my experience, the folk artist responds to an impulse which is largely compulsive: "to make things," or to "tell how it is," or possibly to become a purveyor of some traditional skill. Often, these three motives are inextricably bound together— but occasionally one predominates to the virtual exclusion of the others, as in Ned's case. Ned's art is highly conceptual.

Perception of the creative product as an *aesthetic reality* is unusual among non-academic artists, and that is precisely what makes their work so ingenuous. What is tendered for sale is generally an embodiment of skill or craft, rather than a piece of art work with measured appeal to refined sensibilities. As in the early stages of society itself, there is no self-conscious artistry here, only an expression of feelings and intuitions. Ned Cartledge is possessed of sharply-honed attitudes about religious and social matters, and they are the motive force behind his carvings.

In all of my discussions with Ned, he has never spoken of the "beauty" of a piece, only of its insight into the American or Southern psyche. Unlike Emerson's "transparent eyeball," Ned's vision is a stethoscope placed on the heart of the Super-American, the bigot, faceless government, or the craven evangelical. There is no traditional skill being transmitted here. The idea of making three-dimensional pictures simply emerged from hours spent carving to pass the time as an arbitrator for cotton brokers in Atlanta. Financial return could hardly have been a motive for creating most of the works either, for their subject matter is generally a burr under the saddle for majoritarian Southerners.

Ned's is clearly a voice of dissent, but the issues cover a spectrum of social and moral deportment that is peculiar to a *time* and *place* in which he has lived, and that places him in a context broader than the purely Southern: it addresses some fundamental traits of American tradition. What *is* uniquely Southern is Ned's abiding concern with the ironies of a dualistic racial system or the excesses of an evangelical church. His interest in international problems such as U.S. involvement in Viet Nam or South Africa belie a provincialism often attributed to the Southern viewpoint. Ned pushes beyond the boundaries of region to assert a pragmatism and an old-fashioned patriotism that appear to have strong roots in what John Kouwenhoven has called the Vernacular Tradition.[1]

In his recent *Half a Truth Is Better than None (Some Unsystematic Conjectures about Art, Disorder and American Experience),* Kouwenhoven takes pains to distinguish between the American tradition of the vernacular and those art forms which are widely understood to be folk art. The term "vernacular," he suggests was, "the best I could find to distinguish the

neglected stream of art I was interested in from the folk arts." He goes on to elaborate:

It is my premise that roughly two hundred years ago the idea of democracy, what might be called the democratic impulse, and the technology of manufactured power quite suddenly collaborated to introduce unprecedented psychological and physical elements into man's environment, elements for which it was necessary to find appropriate and satisfying forms. The innumerable, often anonymous acts of arranging, patterning, and designing that went into the creation of those forms constitute the vernacular as I conceive it. In contrast with the folk arts, whose makers are skilled craftsmen following an ancient and traditional sense of design, vernacular designs are evolved without traditional precedents. Their makers are necessarily tyros, since there are no highly developed craft techniques or design standards for shaping new material to new ends.[2]

What immediately sets Ned Cartledge off from the tradition-rooted artist is this eminently American no-nonsense attitude, based on the *functional* realities of a purely utilitarian outlook. Constance Rourke made me aware of the significance of Ned's garden as a symbol of clear-headed practicality in the way she defines the true meaning of culture. According to Rourke, "the original use of the word culture contains its most far-reaching idea: culture is tillage, a fertile medium, a base or groundwork inducing

---

[1] Kouwenhoven, John A., *Made in America*, Newton Center, 1948. p. 15ff.

[2] _____ , *Half a Truth Is Better than None,* 1982. pp. 80-81.

germination or growth in terms of expression."[3] When I was in the garden with Ned one day during spring planting season, I asked him what the neat row of automobile tires was doing planted there. He responded simply that the tire serves as protection for the young plant, as well as mulching around its roots, and meanwhile it is filled with water that is available to the plant as needed. His art (for us, available pure doses of American culture), is as unpreoccupied with genteel conformity as is his garden.

But perhaps it's a mistake to be overly focused on Ned's social consciousness or his sometimes thinly-disguised theological outbursts. It may be that at heart, Ned is a humorist. There are few among his mature works that do not seem to have a wry twist of the sort familiar to students of American vernacular tradition. Usually there is a stereotypical figure of rich or poor, good guy or bad guy, black or white, patriotic or subversive—but there is more than that, there is an unmistakable imprint of the great American institution, the comic strip, in many images produced by Ned's imagination.

Color is administered to the carved

surfaces to get the message across, usually in basic primary colors, or if grass is needed, in a secondary green. Words appear in balloon-like clusters familiar to students of American graphic comic tradition, and one would rarely be tempted to insist that the text detracts from what otherwise would stand as an independent visual conception. But perhaps the most compelling similarity exists in the artist's handling of *time*. Like protagonists of most successful comic strips, Ned's cast of characters are all moving on a life-like stage, and the medium that binds them to reality is the medium of time-lapse. In Ned's work, all of human history may be condensed into the evolution of monkey/man before our eyes, or we may participate in the eternal humiliation of two souls forever poised on the picket fence surrounding Eden.

According to Charles C. Alexander, as early as 1935, "A contributor to the *New Outlook* was hailing comic strips as the 'closest possible approach to a common denominator for the people of the United States,' something that offered 'a more important key to an understanding of the American mind than many other better studied evidences of our national culture.' "[4]

[3] Alexander, Charles C., *Here the Country Lies,* Bloomington, 1980. p. 216.

[4] *Ibid.*

Alexander quotes another essayist of the period as insisting that, "The funnies are the doodles of a nation, a form of visual art that was deceptively crude, like Grant Wood's paintings, and filled with the kind of activism and heroism found in Thomas Hart Benton's murals."[5] But it was the art critic Thomas Craven, according to Alexander, who seized on the "quality of irreverence, that, while not confined to America, flourishes as flower and weed, as in no other land or clime."[6]

Fitting together the warp and woof of Ned Cartledge's vernacular practicality his concern for matters of the spirit, and his ubiquitous sense of humor is part of the refreshing tapestry unfolded in his carving. Kouwenhoven once more throws light on this convergence of seemingly disparate elements of the American tradition when he reminds us that the pioneer student of American humor, Constance Rourke, "showed, for instance, how the comic spirit cooperated to fulfill the biblical dry running through much of the revivalism of the time: 'to make all things news.' Humor, especially the frontier variety, served as a leveling agent, deflating lofty notions and tossing aside all alien traditions, partly out of sheer delight in destruction, but also as a part of the

necessary process of clearing the ground for new growth."[7]

A case in point is Ned's handling of the time-honored mythology of the Banishment from the Garden of Eden in a 1979 carving, which was recently published in *American Folk Art of the Twentieth Century*.[8] I feel assured that Ned would be disappointed that there is no acknowledgement of his bold stroke in portraying God as a Black woman with the Star of David dangling from a chain around her neck and standing in the proverbial Southern watermelon patch. This should push all the buttons of any ethnic or religious conservative, and that to Ned has more humorous significance than theological substance.

Once convinced of Ned Cartledge's mission as a humorist/dissenter with an insider's view of the Southern mind and heart, there still remains the question, "Why carve these images out of wood, and then paint color on the three-dimensional surface?" Alexander goes about as far as we are able toward grasping the many-faceted motivation involved here. Back in the turbulent decade of the '30s, when the mood was in his words, "nationalistic, democratic and folkish," Rourke and others inaugurated the immensely

[5] *Ibid., pp. 216-217.*

[6] *Ibid., p. 217.*

[7] Kouwenhoven, *Made in America,* p. 154.

[8] Johnson, Jay & Ketchum, William C. Jr., *American Folk Art of the Twentieth Century,* New York, 1983, pp. 42-43.

valuable Index of American Design in connection with the now famous Federal Art Project. Writing about the impact of the Index on artists and national consciousness, Alexander quotes a contemporary eulogist who claimed that,"In effect, the Index had revived the original meaning of art by adopting the definition that came down to us from Ancient Greece, where art meant fitting, joining and constructing as well as forming, depicting and representing, and where there was no distinction between the so-called fine arts and the industrial arts."[9]

The Greeks polychromed their marbles in the agora to give them more "life," and it is this engagement of artist and society in the marketplace which the modern separation between fine art and folk has made obscure. I've asked Ned why he didn't just paint pictures, and he responds that it is often only with reluctance that he paints the finished carvings. For Ned, the "life" appears to inform his carvings as a result of *tactile* rather than visual involvement. He takes particular delight in subjects which challenge his feelings for texture, such as old barn siding, brick walls, basketry or even animal fur.

This is no display of virtuosity, I'm

convinced. But rather it lays near the center of Ned's conceptualization of his work, and also at the heart of vernacular consciousness. Kouwenhoven cites an early study by Alan Burroughs comparing American painting with its British counterpart, and notes Burroughs' assertion that among Colonial painters, "What took the place of beauty and consciously artistic structure was simply good eyesight." Kouwenhoven adds, "If one traces the course of American painting thereafter, it becomes clear that the only attitude which is traditional in American art is, as Burroughs concludes, 'dependence on fact.' There are, of course, different kinds of realism: realism of the eye, of the emotions, and of the mind; but there is only one fundamental attitude which permits any kind of realism, and that is respect for the thing seen, the feeling aroused, or the attendant thought."[10] The raw material of Ned's art is *his* world of sensation and idea, and he has ultimate respect for that. What better reason to make it as real as a pocket knife and a few colors will allow?

Dr. Robert F. Westervelt
Chairperson of the Art Department
Gainesville Junior College

[9] Alexander, *op. cit.,* p. 212.

[10] Kouwenhoven, *op. cit.,* p. 172.

PLATES
AND ARTIST'S COMMENTARY

The Flag Waver

In this work I have tried to picture the prototype racist, who is willing to destroy the school system rather than have it integrated, and who is also opposed to press freedom and the right of protest. He flaunts his so-called patriotism by waving a flag, the flag of his narrow, bigoted provincialism above the national flag or interest.

Some thoughts that apply to this situation follow: "The very existence of a group that holds an ideology different from our own creates harsh anxiety in us. Why? Because the very fact that they maintain different beliefs implies ours might be wrong." (Author unknown.) Christopher Morley said: "Thus in all lands do small minds confronted by the unusual, show their distress."

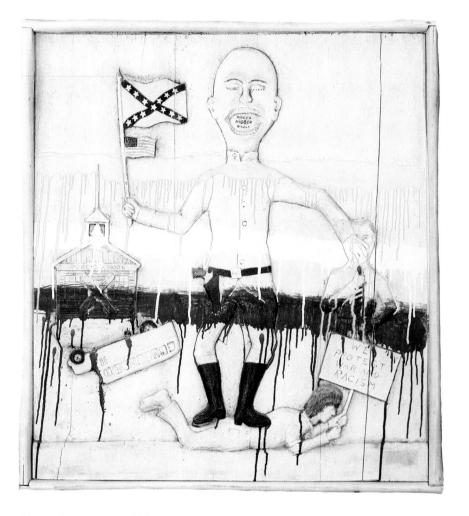

Oil painted wood carving   1970

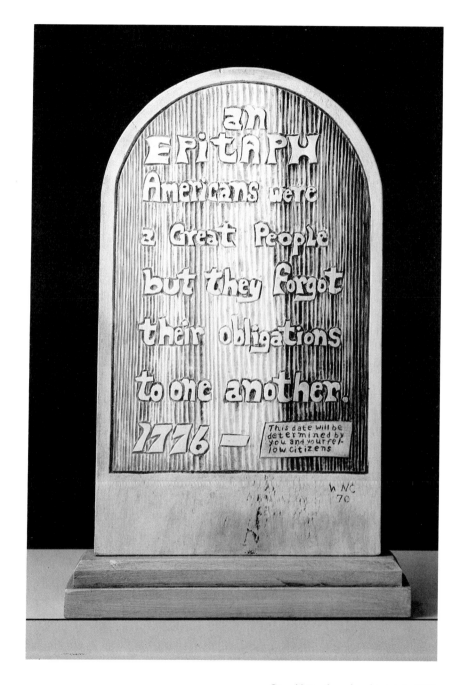

Carved lettered wood—oil painted 1970

Epitaph

This was intended as a warning that this nation has no guarantee that it will always exist as a free and democratic country if we forget the obligations that each citizen has to every other. This idea came from something written by the late John Gardner.

Someone has said that the crisis of democracy is worldwide.

Zbigniew Brezinski asks this question: "Can the institutions of political democracy be adopted to the new conditions sufficiently quickly to meet the crises yet without debasing their democratic character?" As an answer to this question, I thought of the words of a writer of church school books, Sophia Lyon Fahs: "Our hope is with our children and with their children's children, if only they can keep up their courage and keep tender and open to new insights and new habits of thought and action. . . . The history of the universe, as we now understand it, is one long reiterated assurance that the past can be a prologue to a better future if we so wish it to be."

My Lai

This is a sarcastic reaction directed at the people who defended Lt. Calley's conduct at My Lai as acceptable in wartime since his victims were Communists.

I have sardonically portrayed Lt. Calley in a white suit, symbolism for the good guy. His victims all have a "hammer and sickle" imprinted on their bodies to show the excuse for killing them. This work is done in the style of an icon so Calley's defenders could worship their hero.

I suggest that Lt. Calley's conduct was a disservice to all the brave men who served and died in Vietnam. As a tribute to them, I would like to quote from the poem "The Young Dead Soldiers," by Archibald MacLeish:

They say: our deaths are not ours;
They are yours; they will mean what you make them.
They say: whether our lives and our deaths were for peace and a new hope or for nothing
We cannot say: It is you who must say this
They say: we leave you our deaths, Give them their meaning.
We were young they say. We have died. Remember us.

I would like to conclude with words from a letter that Captain Daniel, Calley's prosecutor, wrote to President Nixon:

"When the verdict was rendered, I was totally shocked and dismayed at the reaction of many people across the nation. Much of the adverse public reaction I can attribute to people who have acted emotionally and without being aware of the evidence that was presented and perhaps even the laws of this national regulating the conduct of war. To believe, however, that any large percentage of the population could believe the evidence which was presented and approve of the conduct of Lieutenant Calley would be as shocking to my conscience as the conduct itself, since I believe that we are still a civilized nation."

Oil painted wood carving   20" x 30"   1971

Mother Earth Has Had It

This work was designed to show what over-population is doing to the earth, and what this population has done to exhaust the earth's resources. A prime example of this is Ethiopia where the people have overgrazed, cut the forests and underbrush, and over-cultivated without planning making a virtual desert out of much of their former productive land.

We in the West are guilty of the same thing by polluting our soil and streams, cutting our forests, and over-cultivating our farmland; and it won't be long before we will have exhausted our share of the earth.

It is my belief that uncontrolled population growth may in the long run be as much of a menace to the earth's future as nuclear proliferation. At least there is an effort being made to control nuclear proliferation; whereas, there doesn't seem to be much of an effort to control the earth's population, not by the United States anyway.

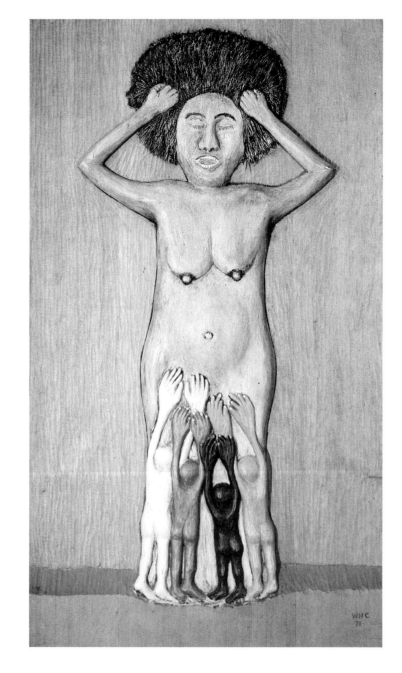

Oil painted wood carving   39" x 22"   1971

Coming Back

This shows a quaint red brick building built by the KKK in the rear of what was their original headquarters at 3155 Roswell Road in Atlanta, Ga. This building referred to above was the warehouse for the Klan, where they did their printing and stored their supplies such as robes, which they sold at the head-quarters in the front.

This building holds memories for me since for ten years I was Manager of the Cotton States Arbitration Board whose offices were located in the building at 3155 Roswell Road. The red brick building in the rear was our warehouse where we stored cotton samples sent to us for arbitration of quality. This building has since been demolished. I wish I could say the same for the Klan mentality.

The title suggests the return of the Klan, and people with the Klan mentality of prejudice, racism, and anti-semitism, and a belief in violence as a means of achieving their goals. Unfortunately, they are still with us. They no longer dress in white robes, though some still do, but in camouflage combat fatigues and arm themselves with automatic weapons.

Someone has said: The notion that making people suffer causes them to abandon their beliefs is a hangover from the days of the Inquisition.

In the collection of the High Museum, Atlanta, Ga.

Acrylic painted wood carving with appliqued parts   26" x 40"   1978

Acrylic painted wood carving   20½" x 20½"   1979

Grin and Bear It

This was done to depict some of President Carter's problems. I tried to inject a little of the "Born again" theme by the wound in the side made by an oil derrick and the country as his cross. The peanut hanging around his neck is like the proverbial millstone, and is symbolic of Carter's image as a mere peanut farmer. The bird on the outline of the country is a vulture which represents many of the wealthy who opposed the President. The little man holding the sign is symbolic of those of us who wish to blame someone else for our country's problems rather than accept the fact that many of these problems are our own fault.

Earl Blackwell—Jimmy Carter:
Carter's successes . . . were forgotten by a people who decided that the absence of a bravura performance . . . signified a weakness.

Garden of Eden

This piece shows a Black female God, with a Star of David necklace, expelling Adam and Eve from the Garden. Depicting God this way was suggested to me by a joke which grew out of the "God is Dead Theory" expounded by an Emory University theologian in the Sixties. The joke went as follows: Two South Georgia farmers met one day. The first farmer greets the second farmer saying, "I've got some good news and some bad news." The second farmer says, "Let me have the good news first." The first farmer says, "God is not dead!" The second farmer asks, "What is the bad news?" The reply was, "She's Black!" (To those that think they must come to God's defense, I find it very presumptuous that some mortal thinks he or she must come to the defense of an Almighty God.)

In the background of the Garden is a T.V. set with the Coca-Cola logo on the screen, which always brings the question, "What does this have to do with the Garden of Eden?" The Garden of Eden was supposed to be "Paradise" and of course anyone should know that there couldn't be paradise without T.V. and Coca-Cola."

In the collection of Dr. Mac Hooton, Seattle, Washington.

Acrylic painted wood carving   20" x 27"   1979

The Magic of Evolution

Acrylic painted wood carving   19" x 49"   1980

This piece is designed to point out the absurdity of "Creationism." The continuity of evolution is interrupted by the magic aspect of creation as related in Genesis. God creating man from dust reminds me of a magician pulling a rabbit out of a hat. (This piece will not enlighten but will infuriate the fundamentalists.)

Paul Kammerer writes: Evolution is not just a fair dream of the last century, the century of Lamarck, Goethe and Darwin: evolution is truth—sober, delightful reality. It is not merciless selection that shapes and perfects the machinery of life; it is not the desperate struggle for survival alone that governs the world, but rather out of its own strength everything that has been created strives upward toward light and the joy of life, burying only that which is useless in the graveyard of selection.

Quoting from David Madden: If you believe the books of the Bible contain all wisdom, it follows that those who are engaged in a search for truth elsewhere are heathen. Repetition and memorization, not investigation, exploration, or questions of clarification, not questions that probe for proof are the cherished educational mode. Nothing remains to learn, discover; it was all over as soon as the ink dried on the books of the Bible. If you believe that you are pure and that all others are evil, it is not difficult to take upon yourself the task of protecting "evil" people from further evil.

In the collection of Mr. and Mrs. Don Childress, Atlanta, Ga.

Defense Umbrella

This piece presents a situation about which I feel very strongly. Here we are thirty years later still keeping troops in a country for which we sacrificed fifty thousand American servicemen and have given billions of dollars in aid. Yet we continue to keep some forty thousand troops at a cost of billions of dollars annually protecting South Korea while they flood this country with their exports of steel, textiles, and other types of goods. These exports cost thousands of taxpaying Americans their jobs, particularly in the textile field. What is so puzzling and frustrating is that I seemed to be in a small minority of people concerned about it at the time I did this piece.

I sent President Reagan a picture of this piece; the White House returned it to me. Of course I should have saved my postage realizing that they suffer from Anti-Communist hysteria. The argument against pulling our troops out of South Korea is that the North Korean Communists would attack. How long do we defend them? I say that those unemployed textile workers wouldn't give a damn.

After I read in *Time* magazine that American banks had some 4½ billion dollars invested in South Korea, plus other investments by American corporations, I could more easily understand but not agree with this policy. I would think, mistakenly of course, that those budget balancers would notice this multi-billion dollar expense.

We hear all this criticism of protectionism, as we are letting a lot of the better paying jobs go overseas. If we believe those people working at McDonald's or some other fast food place for four or five dollars an hour can be taxed enough to pay off the two trillion dollar deficit, we are sadly mistaken.

Oil painted wood carving   24½" x 21"   1981

20

Oil painted wood carving   17" x 18"   1984

The Media Isn't on Our Side

The title came from a statement made by one of President Reagan's aides.

In this piece I tried to address several facets of the Reagan administration. First, let's take the MX missile which Reagan called the "Peacekeeper." My comment on this is a quote of Retired Rear Admiral Eugene J. Carroll: "Calling the MX a peacekeeper is like calling the guillotine a headache remedy." A defense contractor I have pictured as a robber, which in truth they are. Our expenditures on defense have provided the opportunity for them to steal from the taxpayers, a fact to which the Reagan administration seems oblivious. His administration's attempt to manage the news, and prevent the American people from having access to the knowledge of government activities to which they are entitled are legend. The EPA scandal is a prime example of this.

Knock on the Door

This was suggested by an article I read in the newspaper about this older man in New York state. Though a Republican, he frequently called his Republican Congressman complaining about Reagan's policies after Reagan's election. Though he had never threatened the President, one day two Secret Service men appeared at his door and began questioning him; which conduct suggested the Gestapo's visits. This gave me the title and the two Gestapo-like figures. When the ACLU questioned the head of the local Secret Service office, his reply was that "it was necessary to do this sometimes." I searched for a quotation to fit this reply and I found the statement from William Pitt which I thought was appropriate. The fact that I was, certainly among my acquaintances, the only one who regarded this as a serious invasion of a person's rights prompted me to quote Pastor Martin Niemöller:

In Germany they first came for the Communists;
I did not speak because I was not a Communist.
Then they came for the Jews;
I did not speak because I was not a Jew.
Then they came to fetch the workers members of trade unions;
I did not speak because I was not a trade unionist.
Afterward, they came for the Catholics;
I did not say anything because I was a Protestant.
Eventually they came for me, and there was no one left to speak.

I regard this as one of the most eloquent pleas to people of a democratic society that they must be concerned about what is happening to "other people" if they are to maintain our democratic institutions.

Exhibited at the Emory University Human Rights Exhibit in 1983

Oil painted wood carving   18" x 20"   1981

Oil painted wood carving   17" x 20"   1984

Grounded

This was done to emphasize the relative equality of the U.S. and the Soviet nuclear capabilities.

George Keenan, as well as many other experts, accuses our government of "inflating the estimates of Soviet strength" to get more money out of Congress. It has apparently worked very well.

Our China Policy

After completing this work ridiculing our China policy, I read in *Atlanta* magazine a statement by Dean Rusk. "For the United States to attempt to maneuver the Soviets and the Chinese against each other would be childish. Both are too intelligent to let us get away with such a naive maneuver — any more than we would let them do it to us."

I'm not opposed to our opening up diplomatic relations with Red China, I do question our motives. There is an additional comment I would like to make. When Robert Kennedy first advocated opening up diplomatic relations with Red China, he was branded a Communist sympathizer by some. Strangely enough when Nixon advocated and started the process of opening relations with Red China, it was acclaimed a foreign policy triumph.

In the collection of Edward E. Murray, Baltimore, Md.

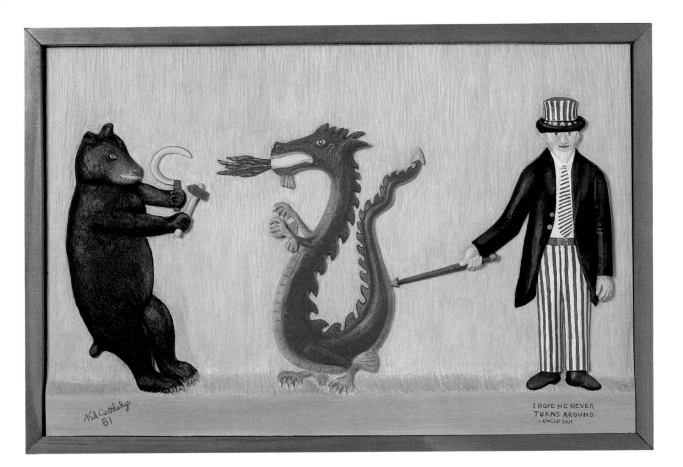

Oil painted wood carving   19" x 27"   1981

Oil painted wood carving 19" x 17½" 1981

Our Kind of Devil

Most of us never seem to be alarmed at the governments of other countries regardless of how cruel and repressive they may be as long as they don't claim to be "Marxist." Following is an excerpt from a "Letter to the Editor" of our local newspaper by Jim P. Cox. "Tell me where were we North American mentors of "peace" and "democracy" when Somoza declared himself president in 1937 by military coup, or stripped the Campesinos of their land for private and personal use; or redirected international relief funds following the Managua earthquake disaster of 1972 into is own organizational coffers." In my opinion it has been the oppressive right wing governments of the "Third World" countries that have given rise to "Communism."

A statement from Robert Kennedy: "If we allow Communism to carry the banner and promise of reform, then the ignored and the dispossessed, the insulted and injured, will turn to it as the only way to get out of their misery."

One of the Leading Economic Indicators

The title originated from the constant reference in the press to the leading economic indicators, but no reference was made to the tragedy of those street people, many of whom because of their lack of education and marketable skills have given up hope and have taken to the street to live. They are statistically forgotten people and are not even included in the un-employment figures.

It also contains a dig at President Reagan's statement to the effect that all the jobless have to do to get jobs is to look in the want ads. The absurdity of this statement is pointed up by a statement made by an unemployed textile worker that I saw on T.V. The mill in which he had worked for forty years was forced to close because of foreign competition. He said, "I don't know how to do nothing else but work in a cotton mill and there ain't no more of them jobs."

Referring to the street people, Dr. John Talbot says, "We are talking not about people who by reason of choice want to be vagabonds or hobos, or some other romantic idea of home-lessness. These people are in the streets because they cannot think straight, make decisions and organize their lives."

In the collection of Stevie and Stanley Sackin, Atlanta, Ga.

Oil painted wood carving   19"x 17½"   1982

26

Oil painted wood carving   19"x 23½"   1982

Trickle Down Economics

The first time I ever heard the phrase "Trickle Down Economics" was during the presidential campaign of 1980. The idea that by tax breaks and incentives for the rich somehow wealth would trickle down to the less fortunate was a revolting theory to me. I have always felt that the rich could take care of themselves, it's the poor who need help. Consequently, I began to think of some way to make a comment on this idea. It was a long process of a couple of years before I came up with what I thought would be an effective critical comment. This piece shows a man in top hat and tails who has stopped his chauffeured Rolls Royce on a bridge of Tax Break Road to relieve himself. Two men, one black and one white, who are fishing in Poverty Creek dressed in blue jeans and undershirts, symbolic of their less affluent condition. The white man extending his hand upward feeling the drops of urine remarks: "I guess this is trickle down economics?" The black man replies, "I don't know nothing about no economics, but I think we're getting pissed on." The relative positions of the rich on top and the poor below represents what some sociologists consider to be an economic trend towards a fragmentation of our society into the haves and have nots, a situation about which we all should be concerned.

This statement by Alex Comfort may sound a bit exaggerated when applied to our society, but I believe it does contain a lot of wisdom:

> It requires no social conscience, only the foresight for the lack of which the French Aristocracy lost their elegant but unemployed heads, to see that our underfed fellow men will not starve to provide us with two pound steaks.

In the collection of the Carrollton Parks and Recreation Dept.

Inconsistencies

This piece as its title suggests points out the inconsistencies of people who proclaim their regard for human life while they support nuclear arms buildup and capital punishment.

In the collection of Stevie and Stanley Sackin, Atlanta, Ga.

Oil painted wood carving   22" x 18"   1984

Oil painted woodcarving   16½" x 31"   1985

It's All a Matter of Perspective

This was done as an educational piece to inform a large portion of the American public who has been taken in by the charm of President Reagan who campaigned on the issue of the ruinous effect of a large deficit and who promised to balance the budget by 1983. He now, as I believe, hypocritically supports a balanced budget amendment, while he has presided over a deficit larger than those of all the other presidents before him combined.

It was somewhat surprising to learn, that in a poll about the budget deficit, that 31% thought the big deficit originated under the Democrats before the Reagan administration. This emphasizes the fact that before citizens of a democratic country can have responsible government, they must inform themselves concerning that government. The popular thing to do in this country is to blame the politicians, particularly Congress, for all our problems, when, as a matter of fact, the voters who do not keep themselves informed and who do not vote intelligently are responsible for the type of government we have. This is a rather obvious observation but it can't be repeated too often.

Some statements of Ronald Reagan in regard to a balanced budget:

"I don't know whether it (a balanced budget) is political or not, but it is absolutely necessary." (1/12/76)

"I believe the budget can be balanced by 1982 or 1983." (9/21/80)

"This administration is committed to a balanced budget and we will fight to the last blow to achieve it by 1984." (9/21/81)

"In the first place, I said that (a balanced budget) was our goal, not a promise." (12/17/81)

Thoughts on Wisdom and Patriotism

Originally this was just a blue owl which I had done just to be a little unconventional. Nobody showed much interest in it. One day it occurred to me to "Finster" it, taking a cue from Reverend Finster who does a lot of writing on his pieces. Though the space was limited, there were some statements I wanted to make about wisdom and patriotism, the owl symbolic of wisdom and the flag motif for patriotism. I quote the statements below:

Wisdom, like beauty is often in the eye of the beholder. Men believe what they wish.

Beware of any person or source that claims to be the fountainhead of all wisdom and truth.

The prevalence of the intolerance of other people's views on religion and politics is very alarming. Waving a flag doesn't a patriot make. The real patriots are those who acknowledge this nation's faults and at the same time try to correct them through the democratic process. The real patriot is as concerned about the rights and well-being of his fellow citizens as he is about his own. A wise man's politics should be based on issues not on personalities.

The very things that have made this country great are now under attack: public schools, religious freedom, and a free press.

You may not consider these statements to be wisdom, but please don't give up searching for it. It's out there somewhere!

In the collection of Greg Simmons, Atlanta, Ga.

Oil painted three-dimensional carving   23" x 11"   1985

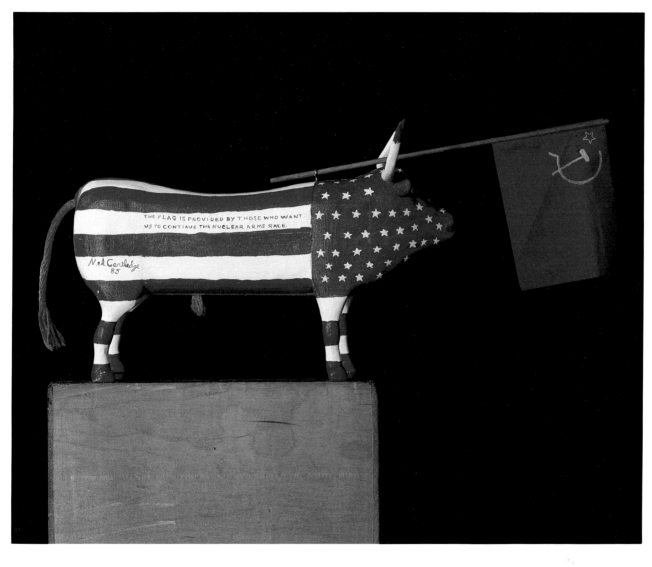

Acrylic painted three-dimensional carving   5" x 13"   1985

Anti-Soviet Hysteria

This piece was inspired by a statement of George Keenan's: We suffer, he agrees from a kind of "Anti-Soviet Hysteria" that converts conventional political rivalry into an Armageddon-like showdown between good and evil.

Words of Thomas J. Watson: The Soviets will never be our friends, on the other hand, they're here on this small planet with you and me, and we've got to learn to live with the Soviets or we're surely going to destroy each other.

In the collection of Stevie and Stanley Sackin, Atlanta, Ga.

Tobacco Mouth

This was inspired by an episode I saw on "Sixty Minutes" as well as all the commercials that one sees on T.V. trying to encourage the use of tobacco and snuff. In spite of the evidence presented by the medical profession, the spokesmen for the tobacco and snuff industry still hypocritically deny there's any proof that these products cause cancer.

This is one of "My Young Peoples Series."

Oil painted three-dimensional carving   15" diameter   1985

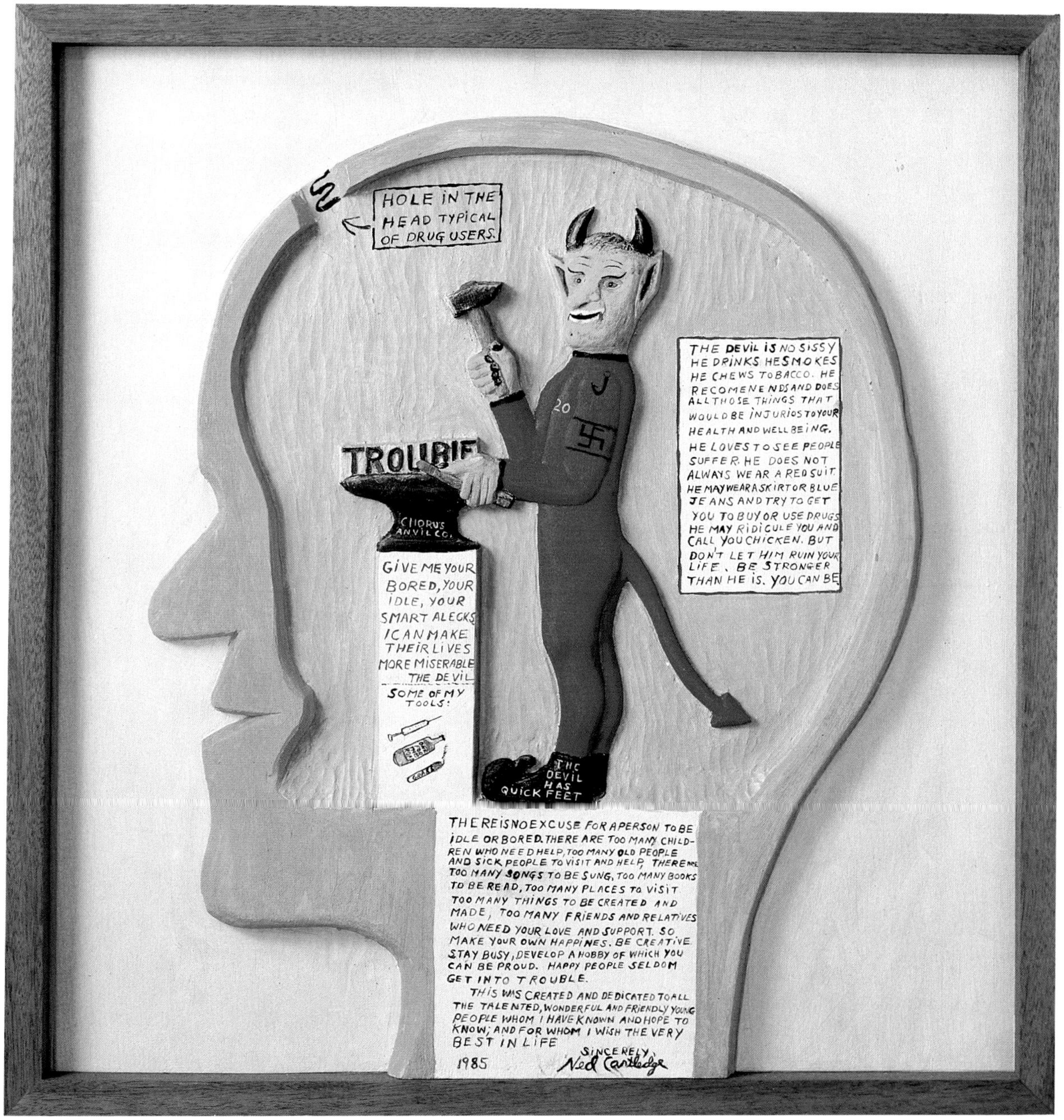
HOLE IN THE HEAD TYPICAL OF DRUG USERS.
THE DEVIL IS NO SISSY HE DRINKS HE SMOKES HE CHEWS TOBACCO. HE RECOMENENDS AND DOES ALL THOSE THINGS THAT WOULD BE INJURIOS TO YOUR HEALTH AND WELL BEING. HE LOVES TO SEE PEOPLE SUFFER. HE DOES NOT ALWAYS WEAR A RED SUIT HE MAY WEAR A SKIRT OR BLUE JEANS AND TRY TO GET YOU TO BUY OR USE DRUGS HE MAY RIDICULE YOU AND CALL YOU CHICKEN. BUT DON'T LET HIM RUIN YOUR LIFE. BE STRONGER THAN HE IS. YOU CAN BE
20
TROUBLE
CHORUS ANVIL CO.
GIVE ME YOUR BORED, YOUR IDLE, YOUR SMART ALECKS I CAN MAKE THEIR LIVES MORE MISERABLE THE DEVIL
SOME OF MY TOOLS:
GRASS
THE DEVIL HAS QUICK FEET
THERE IS NO EXCUSE FOR A PERSON TO BE IDLE OR BORED. THERE ARE TOO MANY CHILDREN WHO NEED HELP, TOO MANY OLD PEOPLE AND SICK PEOPLE TO VISIT AND HELP, THERE ARE TOO MANY SONGS TO BE SUNG, TOO MANY BOOKS TO BE READ, TOO MANY PLACES TO VISIT TOO MANY THINGS TO BE CREATED AND MADE, TOO MANY FRIENDS AND RELATIVES WHO NEED YOUR LOVE AND SUPPORT. SO MAKE YOUR OWN HAPPINES. BE CREATIVE STAY BUSY, DEVELOP A HOBBY OF WHICH YOU CAN BE PROUD. HAPPY PEOPLE SELDOM GET INTO TROUBLE.
THIS WAS CREATED AND DEDICATED TO ALL THE TALENTED, WONDERFUL AND FRIENDLY YOUNG PEOPLE WHOM I HAVE KNOWN AND HOPE TO KNOW; AND FOR WHOM I WISH THE VERY BEST IN LIFE
SINCERELY,
1985
Ned Cartledge

Oil painted wood carving 22"x 21" 1985

The Idle Brain

This is what I call an educational piece part of the series of works which I call "My Young People's Series." It is in the context of the statement below that I have done this work. The aim of this series is to encourage every young person to become a useful citizen and to develop his individual powers to the fullest extent of which he is capable, while at the same time to be engaged in useful and lifelike activities and to be aware of the pitfalls which might befall him on his way to achieve his goals.

Realizing that the writing I have done on the piece may not be legible in the picture, written below will be some of the words on this piece.

Statement to the right of the devil:
The devil is no sissy; he drinks, he smokes, he chews tobacco. He recommends and does all those things that would be injurious to your health and well being. He loves to see people suffer. He does not always wear a red suit, he may wear a skirt or blue jeans and try to get you to buy or use drugs. He may ridicule you and call you "Chicken," but don't let him ruin your life. Be stronger than he is, you can be!

Statement below the devil:
There is no excuse for a person to be idle or bored. There are too many children who need help; too many old people and sick people to visit and help; there are too many songs to be sung; too many books to be read; too many places to visit; too many things to be created and made; too many friends and relatives who need your love and support. So make your own happiness; be creative, stay busy, develop a hobby of which you can be proud. Happy people seldom get into trouble.

This was created and dedicated to all the talented, wonderful and friendly young people I have known and hope to know; and for whom I wish the very best in life.

Nuclear Sand Box

For a long time I had planned to do a piece on nuclear disarmament negotiations. Then I got my inspiration from an article I belatedly read in the January '85 issue of *Esquire* magazine by Ronald Steel about the nuclear armament views of George Keenan, former Ambassador to the Soviet Union, and also an expert on Russia.

The symbolism of the sandbox is to emphasize the childishness of the arms race, as if one child is trying to out do the other without regard to the consequences. Mr. Keenan refers to our "vast addiction" to the arms race and the "almost exclusive militarization of thinking" in Washington about relations with the Soviet Union.

Someone has said, "Tolerance is a boring and dull virtue, yet this is the only force which will enable difference races, classes, and interests to settle down together to the work of achieving peace. Tolerance doesn't mean indifference."

Oil painted wood carving   17½" x 27"   1985

Oil painted wood carving   29" x 15"   1985

Church of the Gullible

This is an obvious criticism of some of the T.V. evangelists, who are supported by the gullible.

Quoted in this piece is a statement made by Thomas Jefferson in 1810, which I believe is applicable to certain T.V. evangelists today. The essence of this quotation is that certain clergymen have perverted the teachings of Jesus to attain wealth and power for themselves.

This statement by Lenny Bruce applies to these people: "Any man who calls himself a religious leader and owns more than one suit is a hustler as long as there is someone in the world who has no suit at all."

David Madden in his essay entitled "The Constitution and the Puritans," in which by his definition equates the term "Puritan" with the fundamentalist, says: " 'We are a nation founded on religion,' boasts the small percentage of religious people who make up the new Puritan minority. We search in vain in the Constitution for a statement that says American democracy is a product of religion. 'We are civic minded,' they declare. Is then a civic-minded person one who violates the spirit of the First Amendment in the name of religious orthodoxy? New Puritans regard citizens who disagree with them as evil and damned and, therefore, undeserving of rights, one has rights as long as one does not dissent.

"With this mentality, the new Puritans are somehow able to think of themselves as the true Americans (not governed, one assumes, by our Constitution, however). This is their country: all others live here by special dispensation.

"Perhaps each member of the silent majority will ask himself or herself, "Do I want to be governed by the convictions of a nonelected, self-appointed faction of citizens? Do I or do I not believe in the democratic, in freedom of expression, in the right of writers to write, teachers to teach, students to read, free of unreasonable, unofficial censoring?"

My Involvement
in Art Work

Some writers and critics call me a folk artist. I call myself a woodcarver.

My work style is usually bas relief wood carvings, which I have painted either in acrylics or oils for a more colorful effect; however, I have done some three-dimensional carvings as well as paintings. I have used various woods in my carvings depending on their availability but principally pine, poplar or basswood.

I do these carvings to make statements on issues and situations which I believe are of importance to the average American. I realize that some of my views are not held by a majority of the electorate but I believe that it is important for minority views to be exposed and respected.

My art is directed to the "man in the street" who, I believe, is often times bewildered by much of what he views in the world of art. I try to express my comments in simple terms under standable to most people. Why make a statement if only a few understand it?

Referring to political art, John Howett of Emory University says, "In the end, art may only be a memorial; it almost never succeeds as a banner, but sometimes it must try." I suspect he is right, so let me say I have created a lot of

memorials; which may mean in the end that my work will be valued only as an historical record of social and political ideas and events.

Quoting from a recent newspaper article about an exhibit of my work: "Peter Morrin, Curator of 20th Century Art at the High Museum said of Cartledge, 'The quality of his work has a lot to do with his own personal qualities of honesty and sincerity, but also with his ability to turn anger into humor, to call attention to wrongs, but to do it in the manner of the great English artist Hogarth. He is really a southern Hogarth.' "

My work is not all political. I also do carvings, relief and three-dimensional pieces of watermelon slices, animals and birds. These are done to support my habit, so to speak, of doing commentary art for which there doesn't seem to be a great demand commercially. My devotion is to humanity and democracy.

I first began carving at the age of nine or ten years; probably whittling would be a more descriptive word. I whittled from wooden boxes easily obtained from grocery stores: pistols, rifles, swords and daggers, things used by young boys in playing out their boyhood fantasies of adventure. The wood from these boxes usually was a soft white pine, which made my mother's paring knife an acceptable tool, as I didn't own a pocket knife until I was twelve years old. The money for my purchase of this knife was earned by working as the water-boy on the construction of the Austell Waterworks system at seventy-five cents an hour.

After I moved to Atlanta in 1930 my carving practically stopped due to a lack of motivation, and to my poor adjustment to "City Life," which was further aggravated by my extreme shyness.

I didn't resume my interest in carving until 1947, the year of my marriage. I jokingly said that when I married, my chain didn't reach very far so I took up woodcarving as a hobby I could carry on at home. Much to my wife's inconvenience, I did this in the kitchen since we lived in a third floor apartment. The things I carved most were small wooden boxes which I made under crude circumstances with few professional tools. These boxes were usually given as gifts, especially carved with something meaningful to the recipient such as a name or initials. One of the boxes I did in those days

was one I called "The Georgia Box," whose purchase by Sidney Guberman, a nationally recognized artist, certainly encouraged me. From the boxes I went to small plaques, fish and birds that I sold at church bazaars usually for practically nothing. A prominent gallery owner introduced me to a friend as a person who does cute little things in wood.

After the box and plaque era, I first carved a panoramic piece called "The Story of Cotton," which I did for myself as a memento of the years spent in the cotton industry. Not wanting to sell this piece but wanting to exhibit it, I entered it in the Piedmont Arts Festival in about 1964, trying to price it so it wouldn't sell. It sold the first day.

The Vietnam War brought a change in the nature of my art work. I began doing work with critical comment on the war, the first being a piece which I called a "wood construction" for the lack of a better description. In 1968 I did a piece on segregation called "The White Fence," which I also describe as a wood construction though it has some carving. In 1969 it was entered in the Savannah Arts Festival, where it received the Second Award. Having had such luck in Savannah, in 1970 I submitted my piece "Under the Cloak of Justice" dealing with eavesdropping and wiretapping; it won "The Best in Show" Award which gave me my first "one man show." It was not a great hit due to the paucity of pieces.

In 1970, I completed a wood carving which I framed in axehandles, symbolic of the racist views held by many at that time. In 1971 it was submitted to the Arts Festival of Atlanta where it received a purchase award. I regard this as one of the strongest pieces I've ever done, though technically it is not one of my best-carved pieces.

This work, exhibited in 1978 at Peachtree Center, was probably instrumental in furthering my art career as it was seen by Judy Alexander who immediately paid me a visit and gave my work a name—folk art. Up until this time I had not known how to describe it.

When I submitted my work for exhibition I never entered in the sculpture category but always entered them as paintings, as they were painted. I had almost given up Art Work with the exception of a few abstract things in which no one seemed interested and justifiably so.

Judy encouraged me to continue my folk or primitive work, even purchasing a piece—a handcarved whiskey cabinet with a western saloon motif. Judy promised me a show at a "Folk Art" gallery. She kept her promise in the fall of 1979 with a one-man show, which was the first time I had exhibited and sold in a commercial gallery.

At the exhibit in 1979, Gudmund Vigtel, director of the High Museum, purchased the first piece I ever sold to a public gallery—a three-dimensional watermelon slice. This almost began a separate career for me; when this was exhibited at the High Museum many people asked me to do watermelons. Realizing that I could not absolutely reproduce the original and that each one would be different, I embarked on making watermelons of painted wood.

I often refer to my work as "not living room art," this was my reaction to a gallery owner who stated that most art is sold to decorators or for the purpose of decoration. Perhaps this is why I still own a great majority of my work.

Since I live frugally on my Social Security and other small sources of income, I can continue to do my social and political comment, the creation of which has been very rewarding to me, especially when it is recognized and approved by persons whom I regard as thoughtful. My work is not done to display my carving or painting skills which at best are mediocre, but to make comments on situations which I consider to be important or relevant.

In 1985 art experts representing the French Ministry of Culture selected eleven pieces of my work to be exhibited in France as part of the "Atlanta in France" exhibit sponsored jointly by the City of Atlanta and the French Ministry of Culture. Seeing my work exhibited in Paris and Toulouse as well as the trips to these cities (provided by the sponsors) was an especially exciting and rewarding experience for me.

My 1985 exhibit at the Unitarian Universalist Congregation Gallery gave me an opportunity to have on display 39 pieces of my work.

I was born in Canon, a small farming community in northeast Georgia, October 1, 1916. I was the fifth child of six children my family had, sandwiched in between an older sister and a cute flaxen-haired younger sister.

In the summer of 1923 when the bank failed at which my father was cashier, my father, mother, three sisters and I moved to three rented rooms on Pine Street. My two brothers, the oldest of the children, remained in Canon with my grandmother. My great uncle Judge had driven us to Atlanta in a big long Studebaker touring car with all the family belongings which consisted of clothing, bed linens and dishes packed in boxes. The thing I remember most vividly, in addition to the street cars which I had never seen before, were the innoculations that all of us children had to take before entering school.

Shortly after school started, my great uncle, who was president of the other bank in Canon, persuaded my father to return there to assume the job of cashier at this bank. It seems that the directors had said that they were not willing to reopen the bank unless Tom Cartledge, my father, was to be cashier. I took considerable pride from the fact that in later years when I would return to Canon, older men upon meeting me would say, "Oh! You're Tom Cartledge's boy; your father was one of the most honest and upright men I ever knew." This bank too failed as the boll weevil had rendered most of the cotton crop a failure, cotton being the prime cash crop in this area. The Depression came to the rural areas of Georgia long before the crash of 1929.

My grandmother and mother were members of the local Universalist Church, which was considered by many in the community, due to their ignorance, a church that didn't believe in God because the philosophy of the church was that there were other sources of truth and wisdom than the Bible.

In 1925 my family moved to Austell, Georgia, where we ran the local hotel. Two of my pieces have addressed experiences there: "My First Day at a New School" and "Austell Waterworks." I was a good student at the Austell School which I attended through the first half of the eighth grade.

From there we moved in 1930 to Atlanta where my mother operated a boarding house. Shortly after the move, my father lost his job for having voted for Herbert Hoover, so his boss told him. The boss told my father he was reluctant to do this but was ordered to do so by the higher-ups who had found out my father's vote. In Atlanta I enrolled in O'Keefe Junior High School and was placed in the "accelerated group" which enabled me to complete one and a half year's work in one year. After about a year

and a few sacks of Red Cross flour, which my father's friends prevailed on him to reluctantly accept because of his unemployment, my father was rehired at his old job. In those days I had two pairs of pants, one on and one in the wash.

Something happened to me in 1932 on a summer vacation to my grandmother's which had an impact on me the rest of my life. Though my father, mother, and grandmother had segregationist views, as most people in the rural South did in those days, they never, that I can recall, expressed their opinions openly in front of the children. My father who was a shy, mild mannered man was strongly opposed to the KKK.

My grandmother had converted the unusually large kitchen of her house, in which she had formerly operated the local boarding house, into a small dry goods and grocery store. She enjoyed a good relationship with blacks who spent their meager wages in the store, in spite of the fact that some would say their bosses recommended other stores. Grandmother made a rule of giving fair weights to the small amounts of side meat, coffee, sugar, cheese and other staples which were usually bought in five and ten cent amounts. Since white men were paid fifty cents a day for farm work, I suspect that blacks only got maybe forty cents. Frequently after making their purchases and obviously out of money, my grandmother would go to the candy counter, pick out a small bag of candy and give it with the statement, "Here's something for the children." She did this knowing full well that would be the only way the children would ever be able to enjoy candy.

There arrived in town that summer from Detroit, where they were employed in the auto industry, several children and in-laws of a black farmer, who had the ambition and courage to leave an impossible situation. To further irritate the racists who were unemployed and on what little relief was available, these blacks appeared to be prosperous and were driving a large black La Salle sedan. You can very well imagine the envious and hate-filled comments made, even by my grandmother.

One day the La Salle stopped in front of Grandmother's store and two black women got out and entered the store. I could see the antagonism in my grandmother's face as one of them addressed my grandmother as follows: "Miss Mary, we would like to buy a few groceries." My grandmother replied coolly, "Okay, what do you want?" After naming several canned goods, one of them asked, "Do you have any country butter?" My grandmother replied, "Yes we do." We kept a cow which I usually took care of and milked so that I could have the milk and buttermilk I liked. We always had more butter than we could eat, selling the surplus in the store. It was not unusual in those days for butter to be tainted with bitterweed, which rendered it unpalatable, but this condition could be easily detected by its pungent odor. As Grandmother placed the butter patty on the counter, one of the women asked politely, "May I smell it?" My grandmother exploded saying hatefully, "Down here niggers don't smell white folks' butter before they buy it!" Without a word, the two women walked out of the store, leaving the butter and the canned goods on the counter.

I was so embarrassed at my grandmother's conduct, I almost cried, which I have always had a propensity to do in response to very emotional situations.

Though this incident never diminished my love for my grandmother, it certainly made me question her wisdom which I had admired so much prior to this. I just never could get out of my mind the cruelty of this incident and segregation in general.

I was a fairly good student when I returned to Atlanta and Boys' High in 1934, making the honor roll for a couple of semesters. I was graduated in 1935.

Something happened in my senior year which gave me an opportunity to express my faith in our system of government. From junior high, I developed an intense interest in our government and politics, especially as it related to the organized labor movement. I entered an American Legion Essay Contest for which the subject to be addressed was "Good Citizenship in 1935." Despite the discouraging remarks by one of my friends who had also entered the contest, I submitted my essay. I will admit that my friend was a superior student in English Composition who later became a published poet and professor of literature at Florida State University, but he lacked my dedication to the subject. I won the first prize for all the senior high schools in the city, which was a medal and twenty dollar cash prize.

After graduation, as scarce as jobs were, I obtained a job by joining the Carpenters Union as an apprentice at which trade I worked for about six months. Later through the influence of my brother-in-law who was employed by this company, I obtained a job in the cotton classing department of Anderson, Clayton and Co. which was at the time the world's largest cotton merchandizing firm.

My employment with them was interrupted by World War II in which I served as an enlisted man and an officer. My combat duty was in the European theater where I served as a company executive officer in a chemical mortar battalion which supplied high explosive and smoke screen support for infantry divisions. While we were attached to the 82nd Airborne, I witnessed concentration camps and other atrocities of the Germans, such as the Garelegen incident, after the fact. Some years later I would participate in the "Witness to the Holocaust" program sponsored by Emory University which appeared in several segments on television.

I returned to my job at Anderson Clayton after the war. At first there was much bitterness among the returning veterans because of the management's lack of concern for us.

In 1946 I met my future wife, Amy,

a widow with two daughters by a previous marriage, and we were married a year later. She and I also had two daughters.

In 1960, I began a career as a cotton broker, selling cotton to mills for cotton merchants. I had modest success at this but when offered the position of manager of the Cotton States Arbitration, an arbitration service for the cotton industry, I accepted. Since this job was much like a fireman's, we were often not busy and I devoted a great deal of time to my wood carving and did a lot of reading which helped me to develop my views on religion and politics. I served as manager from 1963 to 1973 when the associations which sponsored the Board moved it to Memphis. Since I was working as a part-time hardware salesman at the Sears Buckhead store, I applied for a permanent job and was accepted. I retired a few months after reaching age sixty-five in 1982.

My retirement years have been quite active as I have two reciprocal hobbies; I garden in suitable weather, and do my art work at night or during cold or inclement weather.

I have often pondered as to what influenced me to begin whittling as I was a whittler before I was a carver.

As I recall my early boyhood days, when I was six or seven years old, I remember seeing farmers and local workmen sitting on crates or their haunches in front of a store near my grandmother's house where I lived. These men seemed to have very sharp knives and would frequently hone them on the bottom of their shoes as they whittled on a piece of board from a packing crate. Most of them whittled, making shavings. However, there was one man named Ben who was different; he always whittled little axes. After he got the shape of the axe as he wanted it, he would sit there scraping the wood with the knife blade until it had a very smooth finish.

One day as I walked past these men picking my way through the tobacco juice on the dirt sidewalk, Ben called to me rather abruptly, "Come here, boy!" Being extremely shy, I hesitated and he said, "Don't be afraid, I have something to give you." He gave me a little axe which pleased me very much. Thanking him, I excitedly turned and ran home to proudly show my mother my gift.

As I think back on this, I credit this experience of watching Ben whittle with developing my interest in working with wood.

As I have often thought, there is a lesson to be learned from this experience. Some people go through life just whittling, making shavings or debris, while others expending the same amount of effort create or produce useful or artistic things.

Woodcut   1986   Ned Cartledge

Exhibitions of Ned Cartledge's art:

One Person Exhibitions:

1987   "Ned Cartledge: Comment and Satire,"
Georgia Museum of Art, Athens

1985   Unitarian-Universalist Congregation
Gallery, Atlanta

1979   Alexander Gallery, Atlanta

Group Exhibitions:

1986   "Humor," Nexus Contemporary Art
Center, Atlanta
"Visual Arts—the Southeast," Atlanta

1985   "Birmingham Biennial," Birmingham
Museum of Art, Birmingham
"Arts Festival of Atlanta," Atlanta
"Carrollton Juried Exhibit," West
Georgia State College, Carrollton
(Purchase Award)

1984   "Arts Festival of Atlanta," Atlanta
"USA/Portrait of the South," Palazzo
Venezia, Rome, Italy
"Georgia Artsts: 1984," Decatur
(Merit Award)

1983   "Birmingham Biennial," Birmingham
Museum of Art, Birmingham
"Human Rights," Emory Museum of
Art, Atlanta

1982   Theatrical Outfit, Atlanta
"Arts Festival of Atlanta," Atlanta
Jay Johnston Gallery, New York

1981   "Arts Festival of Atlanta," Atlanta

1972   "Arts Festival of Atlanta," Atlanta
(Purchase Award)

1970   "Savannah Arts Festival," Savannah
(Best in Show Award)

1969   "Savannah Arts Festival," Savannah
(Second Award)

Collections:

Atlanta, Georgia: High Museum of Art
Austin, Texas: Lyndon Johnson Library
Bath, England: John Judkyn Memorial
Carrollton, Georgia: City of Carrollton Art
Collection
New York, New York: Chase Manhattan Bank
Santa Fe, New Mexico: Museum of Inter-
national Folk Art
plus private collections in Georgia, Maryland,
New York, Ohio, and Washington

Index of Plates

To afford another person the opportunity to have his voice heard, even though one may not agree with all he says or anything he says, certainly exemplifies a commitment to democratic ideals. The financial sponsors of this book have provided me the opportunity for the realization of one of my dreams, for which I will be eternally grateful.

STEVIE AND STANLEY SACKIN
THE MAYOR'S FELLOWSHIP AWARD
LOIS AND RICHARD ROSENTHAL
FRANCES AND EDWARD E. MURRAY
DR. MAC HOOTON
CHERYL AND BRADLEY CRUICKSHANK
MS. ADRIENNE CLEERE
MARY AND JOE YOUNG
MARY AND DICK McLENNAND
    AND FRIENDS
FROM THE 89th CHEMICAL MORTAR
    BATTALION ASSOCIATION
MRS. CHARLOTTE FERST
MARTHA AND JIM SWEENEY
SYLVIA AND JIM KORTAN
JAY CROUSE

My appreciation is extended to the following individuals who contributed their time and talents to this project.

FRED DUBOSE
KATHY EGAN AND SHIRLEY COOKS,
    THE ATLANTA BUREAU OF
    CULTURAL AFFAIRS
DONALD D. KEYES
CLIFTON MEADOR AND LOUISE SHAW,
    NEXUS CONTEMPORARY
    ART CENTER
SANDY TEEPEN
TOM TEEPEN
VIRGINIA TYSON
BOB WESTERVELT